‖‖‖ ‖ ‖‖‖‖‖ ‖ ‖ ‖‖‖‖‖‖‖‖‖‖‖‖‖ ‖‖ ‖‖‖

W9-COL-186

Bicycling Books®

RECONDITIONING THE BICYCLE

by the editors of *Bicycling* magazine

Text and Photos by Richard Jow

Copyright © 1979 by Rodale Press, Inc.

All rights reserved. No part of this publication may be reproduced or transmitted in any form or by any means, electronic or mechanical, including photocopy, recording, or any information storage and retrieval system without the written permission of the publisher.

Printed in the United States of America on recycled paper, containing a high percentage of de-inked fiber._
                    Book series design by K. A. Schell
Library of Congress Cataloging in Publication Data

Jow, Richard.
    Reconditioning the bicycle.

    (Bicycling books series)
        1. Bicycles and tricycles—Maintenance and repair.
I. Bicycling (Emmaus, Pa.) II. Title. III. Series.
TL430.J68   629.28'8'72   79-17423
ISBN 0-87857-285-6 paperback

                10   paperback

Contents

Introduction

The Bicycle Manufacturers Association of America states that there are approximately 100 million 10-speed bicycles in this country. Maybe more. To be sure, this raw statistic is readily confirmed on a spring or summer day. Bicycles appear from nowhere and take to the streets.

Another side to this rosy picture is that millions of derailleur bikes, owned by adults and children alike, are simply not used. After the initial enthusiasm a new bike brings, the owner frequently parks the machine when the slightest trouble occurs. More than one bike shop mechanic has estimated that half the bikes parked in garages or basements need little more than minor adjustments and repairs.

An economist who knows, would tell us that the bicycle is one of the best investments a consumer can make today. The money saved on gasoline and parking tolls would pay for a $200 bike in less than a year. A bike is an investment that will last. What other consumer product will last you 10 years or more—even if you take care of it?

Many have called the bike the last democratic machine. More appropriately, it is one of the few remaining modern-day machines that individuals can actually repair. Bicycle repair is relatively simple and within the grasp of all.

Reconditioning the Bicycle will not show you how to buy a bike; but it will show you how to overhaul your old one. The first part of the book offers a step-by-step account of taking the bike apart, preparing it for painting, painting, reassembling and adjusting the components.

The middle chapters of the book demonstrate how you can lighten your bike for better performance by selectively replacing

Introduction

major components, particularly on the revolving parts of the bike.

The last part of the book deals with some basic repairs and adjustments, including repairing a broken stem, wrapping and padding the handlebars, repairing frayed cables, and overhauling hubs and freewheels.

Written by Richard Jow, an expert mechanic who tested all the procedures in the workshop, this book is full of tips and hints to help make your bike run troublefree.

Reconditioning the Bicycle is designed to help you overhaul and improve the performance of your present bike; to help keep it on the road as long as possible.

James C. McCullagh
Editor
Bicycling magazine

Part One
Renovating the Bicycle Frame

Bicycle Tools

The most indispensable things to have before putting what you read in this book to practice will be the proper tools to perform each different job. I have described alternate methods of accomplishing jobs within the different sections but nothing makes it easier than having the tool meant to do the job at hand.

Listed and shown are some of the more specialized tools which will make your reconditioning job much easier.

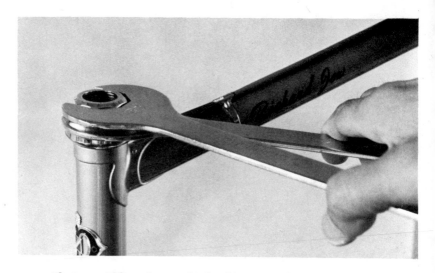

Photo 1: Although not absolutely essential, two thin 32-mm wrenches make headset adjustment much easier. The wrenches are squeezed together when tightening or loosening to prevent the steering tube from twisting and for better control.

Photo 2: The disassembly of a hub requires a set of thin cone wrenches to fit the cone and locknut. The proper way to use these is as shown; squeeze one against the other to avoid skinned knuckles.

Photo 3: Each make of crankset has its own crank remover tool of which some are interchangeable. Be sure to give your dealer the make and model of your crankset to obtain the right tool. The Dura-Ace tool shown also has a socket for the crank bolt.

Photo 4: A fixed cup wrench is indispensable if a bench vise or a large wrench is not available. This tool has a long handle for the higher torque required in tightening and loosening the cup.

Photo 5: Unless you have an extra pair of hands to help out, a lockring wrench and pin wrench will cut installation time in half. The pin wrench is held stationary for the proper adjustment while the lockring is tightened.

Photo 6: To loosen the freewheel, a remover tool is required. There is a different model for each make and sometimes a different one for different models within the same line. Know the make and model of your freewheel before buying. Either clamp the tool in a bench vise and turn the wheel or use a long-handled wrench to loosen the freewheel. Be sure to keep from damaging the freewheel by tightening the quick-release on the tool before applying pressure.

Photo 7: The type of spoke wrench used depends on individual preference. Try the different ones in your hand and see which one feels right for you.

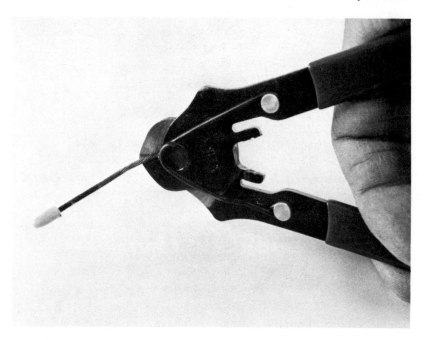

Photo 8: A pair of cable cutters will prevent frayed ends by cleanly severing the cable instead of squashing the cut as when a pair of wire cutters is used. The pair shown, by Maeda Sun Tour, is very reasonable and more than adequate for normal use.

Stripping the Bicycle

To begin, remove the brakes from the front fork and the seatstay bridge. As you do this, check the cable for fraying or worn spots, particularly where they enter the cable housing and where the cable passes the rear adjusting barrel on centerpull brakes. (Start a list of things you'll need to replace so you'll only need to make one trip to the bike shop.) Before laying the brakes aside, see if the blocks are worn; if they are, add them to the replacement list. Check the yoke cable on centerpulls, too.

Remove the handlebar and stem by backing off on the stem bolt about ¼ inch. To keep from damaging the finish, get a piece of wood at least one inch thick and rest it on top of the bolt. Give the piece of wood a sharp whack with a hammer. Be sure to hold the bars up; otherwise, when the tension is released from the expander, the stem will drop into the steering tube, scratching the finish of the stem.

The chain must be removed with a chain rivet extractor. If you don't have one of these, get one. It will come in handy if you plan to do any of your own maintenance work. This is the only tool that will get that chain off for you unless you're working on a 3-speed. If this is the case, look for the master link and pry the locking clip off. When you get a rivet tool, the dealer should have instructions for its use.

Next remove the cranks and chainwheels. To do this, you'll have to make a simple block to hammer on to keep from ruining the bottom bracket bearings, races and crank spindle. After you've made the block (see figure 1 on page 14), lean the bike against a wall and loosen the cotter pin locknut until a bit of the threaded end shows. Place the crank of the bike on the V-section of the block, and with the threaded end of the cotter pin at 12 o'clock, place the piece

Photo 9: Unscrew the expander bolt about ¼ inch, place a block of wood on top of the bolt and hold onto the bars at the same time, then give it a sharp whack with a hammer to release the tension and the stem will come out of the fork tube.

Photo 10: Make yourself a block and use as shown in this photo. Loosen the cotter pin nut until the face of the nut is flush with the end of the cotter pin. Insert the block and strike with a hammer.

of wood used in stem removal on top of the cotter pin nut. Give it a solid whack or two with a hammer until the pin comes loose. Repeat on the other crank.

If you don't have a lockring wrench to loosen the lockring on the adjustable cup of the bottom bracket, a screwdriver driven by a hammer is a workable substitute. Once the adjustable cup is loosened and taken off, take care to count the number of ball bearings that are removed from that side. Next remove the crank spindle. Most people don't have a fixed cup wrench, and for this reason most people will replace everything in a bottom bracket except the fixed cup. If you don't have this wrench, here is an easy way to get by without it. Get a bench vise, a nut and bolt and two flat washers. It will make this operation easier if the frame is bare of all else, so put it off until last.

First, measure the thickness of the jaws of your vise and the width of your bottom bracket. Add these two dimensions together and add another ¾ inch. Next, get a ½-inch bolt the length you've just computed and two large flat washers whose diameters are larger than the bottom bracket diameter; also get a nut. Insert the bolt through the bottom bracket and set the assembly up (as shown in figure 2) with the jaws of the vise clamped to the fixed cup. Tighten the bolt until you can feel the nut drawing up fairly snug. Now turn the frame until you break the grip of the fixed cup, loosen the nut a little and turn the frame some more until the fixed cup is loose. Then take the whole thing apart, and the fixed cup will spin off freely. Be sure to check the threading of the cup before you start turning so you'll be turning in the right direction.

Check the bearing surfaces of the crank spindle, adjustable cup and the fixed cup while this item is still in the bottom bracket. If any one shows signs of wear, replace it. The bearings should be replaced no matter what—I replace mine at least once a year. Take one of the old ball bearings to your bike shop and match the size. Remember, there are different grades of loose ball bearings; get a grade 7 to 10. Ten is the best grade, and it's worth the extra two to three cents a ball. In fact, buy 100 if you can. It will be cheaper, and you will have enough for at least four changes.

Everything else should be fairly easy to remove. The only other problem you might encounter is that you will require, in most cases, a 6-mm allen wrench to remove the mounting bolt of the rear derailleur.

Keep everything together so you won't have any difficulty in locating the small parts when it comes time to put things back together.

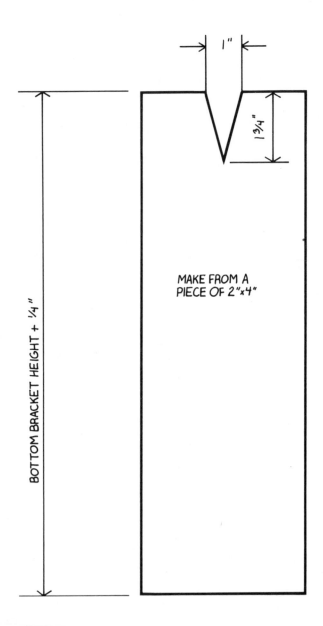

Figure 1: Wooden block to be used in removal of cranks and chainwheels.

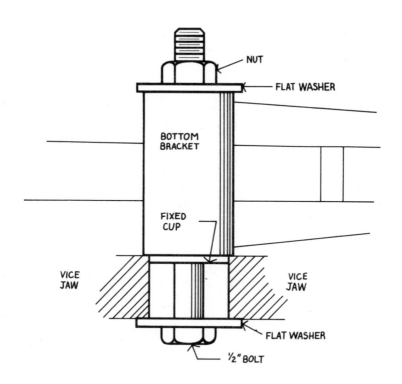

Figure 2: Procedure for removal of crank spindle.

Preparation for Painting

Now we'll prepare the frame for the actual painting.

First, make sure every bit of grease and oil is off the frame. Take some lacquer thinner on a soft clean cloth and wipe down the entire frame. Be particularly thorough around the bottom bracket, head tube, front fork tips and dropouts. Cleanliness is the key to successful painting; the least amount of dirt or oil on the frame will affect the adherence of the paint. If the frame is not clean, the paint will soon start blistering and chipping.

After you've made sure all the dirt and oil have been removed, hang the frame in your garage or workshop. Tie some twine around the seatpost clamp, through ceiling anchors and down to the headset locknut. To achieve this last anchorage, loosen the headset locknut and tie the twine around the fork tube. Tighten the nut again so there's no chance of the twine slipping off.

Choose a place to hang the frame where you'll have unobstructed access. Remember, you must be able to leave the bike here for a week or two where it won't be moved and where foot traffic won't create any dust while the paint dries.

You might try what I tried. I used my six-foot stepladder, which has a shelf for paint cans. I hung the frame from this shelf, making the whole thing portable.

Once you have the frame hung at a workable height, take some ¾-inch masking tape and old newspaper and mask off all the chromed parts so paint isn't inadvertently sprayed where it isn't wanted. The races of the headset can be taped off without any newspaper. Be sure to tape off the bottom bracket opening on the adjustable cup and fixed cup side if you've removed these; if not, tape the fixed cup completely. After you've done this, the only thing that will be showing that you don't want paint on should be the medallion on the head tube.

Photo 11: You can move the whole setup outside for the sanding and move it inside when ready to paint. The shop is left free of airborne dust particles.

Photo 12: Mask off the chrome portions of the frame.

Next, sand and smooth out any of the frame's existing nicks, scratches and chips so they won't appear on the new paint job. Take some fine sandpaper, 00 grit or finer, and feather out all the blemishes so there isn't a sharp outline showing through. After you've gone over all of the blemishes, give the entire surface to be painted a going-over with the sandpaper to create a toothed or

Photo 13: The rear pannier carrier clamp has dug into the paint and will reflect through to the new paint if not sanded and feathered out.

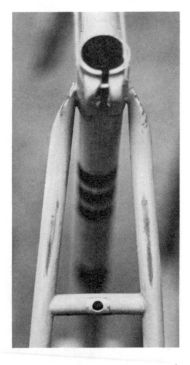

Photo 14: This is what the blemish should look like after feathering.

gripping surface for the new paint. It's not necessary to strip the old paint off and reprime before painting. However, if you're going to be redoing your frame for the second time, I would suggest that the frame be stripped down to at least the base coat or original paint before repainting. I recommend this very strongly as too many coats of paint tend to make the surface coat too soft and prone to chipping and cracking.

The medallion on the headset should now be covered so that it isn't painted over. Take a very small brush and some of the liquid paste wax used for automobiles and lightly paint over the medallion, taking care not to get any wax on the head tube itself.

Photo 15: Carefully brush on several coats of liquid wax to protect the head tube medallion.

You can remove the medallion altogether and rerivet it later with pop rivets, but for this you would need the correct size rivets and a special tool.

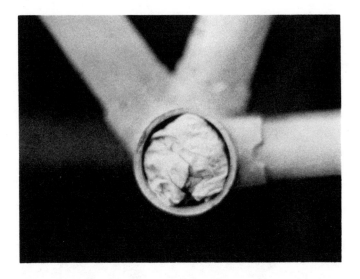

Photo 16: To prevent the bottom bracket threads from becoming clogged with unwanted paint, stuff a rag in just far enough to cover all the threads. Be careful of both sides.

Painting the Bike

In the past, I've found lacquer paint to give the best results as far as do-it-yourself paint jobs are concerned. However, due to air pollution standards in California, lacquer paints are no longer available unless certain conditions are met regarding where and how they are to be used.

If you can get lacquer in your area, go ahead and use it as it will be more durable. Also, you'll have more choices of metallic finishes with lacquer.

By now I hope you have a fairly good idea of what color you're going to use, so go down to your local paint store and see if what you want is available. When you've decided, get one or two 12- to 16-ounce cans. Metallic colors are available at your automotive parts store. This finish involves a two-step process, so you'll have to get both the base color and the transparent, tinted finish color. Read the labels on the cans to see what you need.

When you're satisfied with the tooth in the old paint, prepare the work area where you will be spraying by sprinkling the floor with water to settle the dust. Or, thoroughly vacuum the room and leave it for about a half hour to allow any airborne dust to settle.

Upon reentering the room, be sure not to move about unnecessarily and disturb the dust. Now before actually painting, take a clean lintless cloth and some more lacquer thinner and wipe the sanded portions of the frame until there is no loose sanded paint showing in the rag.

Read the label directions on the spray can once again and follow them. Keep the nozzle 12 inches away from the frame when you're spraying and move your whole arm, keeping the nozzle parallel to the member you're painting. Go over the member lightly with each pass so you don't apply too heavy a coat and get runs. It's better to waste a little paint than to get runs and be forced to strip the frame and start all over again. You'll have to do this if you're using the metallic finishes. There's almost no way to get an even color with the conventional methods of wet-sanding the runs and respraying.

Provide plenty of light in the work area so you won't miss painting any parts in shadow, and have plenty of ventilation.

After you've finished with the spraying, leave the frame alone for at least an hour for the paint to dry. Then go back and very cautiously strip off the masking tape and newspaper. The frame should be left in isolation for a week to insure proper curing and hardening. I've found with any less time the hardness is questionable.

During the week's time pick out a color that complements the primary color of the frame and pick up a small bottle of it at your local hobby shop; they stock the lacquers used for the finishing of model airplanes and boats. At the same time get a very fine, pointed, sable's hair brush. With this you'll line the lugs and the joints between the chrome and the new paint. Some people try to use a stripping brush for this operation, but it's too hard to control on the intricate outlines of some lugs. With a round, pointed, bristled brush, the only thing you need to concentrate on for the correct line width is the pressure. No matter which way you move the brush, the

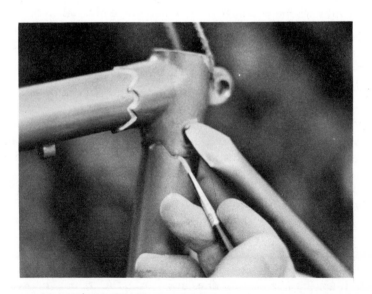

Photo 17: Use a fine, sable's hair brush to line the lugs. A contrasting color will make them stand out.

width will be uniform. But do practice a bit to learn the characteristics of the brush before starting on the frame itself.

When the outlining is done and has dried completely and thoroughly, get a worn-out toothbrush and remove the wax from the head tube medallion or re-rivet it on if you have removed it.

The very last thing to do is to take some wax and give the newly painted frame a thorough waxing. Because of the precautions you've taken, there shouldn't be any roughness in the finish due to dust, but if there is, take a very small amount of rubbing compound and carefully and lightly rub down the finish coat of paint. Then give it a good wax job.

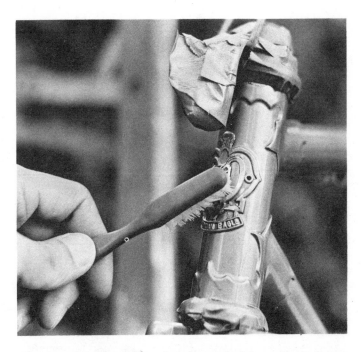

Photo 18: An old toothbrush and a toothpick are the tools to use to remove the unwanted paint from the head tube medallion. Note the masked-off headset bearing races.

Reassembling the Bike

Now we'll start to reassemble the bike.

By this time I hope you have determined which parts are worn and have gotten replacements for them.

One of the first components I reassemble is the bottom bracket set. On most steel cottered cranksets, and some alloy cotterless cranksets, the bottom bracket is not protected with a liner as some of the more expensive sets are. I'll make a liner for the bikes I work on if the bracket doesn't have one. It's a simple thing, doesn't cost anything, and it works.

Cut the ends of an aluminum can off, then snip along the length of the can so that you have a rectangular piece of aluminum. Next, measure the dimension between the threaded portion of the bracket shell and cut a strip of aluminum around the circumference of the original can to fit. Don't worry about the length as the ends will overlap to take care of the excess. Be careful not to end with a piece which is too short. The holes, where the seat tube, down tube and chainstays join, are what we want to cover. This will prevent any stray or loose metal or dirt particles from falling into the bearings. I also stuff a wad of foam rubber down the seat tube to prevent dirt or moisture from infiltrating that opening.

Coil the piece of aluminum enough to insert it into the bottom bracket shell. Make sure that the seam formed by the overlapping ends is on the bottom. Be certain that you've inserted it far enough so that it butts against the fixed cup. Look in and see if it covers all the holes it's supposed to. If not, cut a piece big enough to do the job. After you're satisfied, screw on the adjustable cup to check that the aluminum isn't too wide.

In packing the new bearings use a good, light grade of lithium-base grease. The lithium forms a tenacious bond between the lubricant and the metal surface, even if the parts get wet. This doesn't mean that if you do get water in the bearings that you can just leave them. If I suspect there's water in the bearings and races I always clean and repack.

I've been using a lithium-base, white grease by Sta-Lube for several years and it's easily obtainable at most auto-supply stores. Another choice is the Schwinn grease available from your local Schwinn dealer, or the grease by Campagnolo, Shimano, Gipiemme and Phil Wood.

When repacking, apply a fair amount of grease on the race or cup, then drop the required number of ball bearings onto the race; the grease will hold these in place while you insert the axle. Repeat for the other side, then carefully screw on the adjustable cup. The adjustment for the right amount of free play is something that cannot be readily described; it's all a matter of feel. Tighten your cup finger, then spin the axle. If it's too tight, back off and tighten a bit more. After a couple of tries you'll get the hang of it.

I normally leave the chainwheels and cranks off until I get the wheels and bottom cable guide on. It keeps them from getting in the way.

You should have the hubs disassembled, cleaned and repacked. The front wheel is the easiest to work on, and if you've never taken one apart before, tackle this one first. You'll need a couple of cone wrenches to loosen the axle locknut and cone. These are thin wrenches; one can slip past the other when being turned. Normally they are sized from 13 to 16 mm and will fit most hubs. I've found some cheap, stamped-out steel wrenches which do the job as well as the more expensive cone wrenches will.

When you begin, it's best to remove the locknut and cone from only one side. Leave the opposite side intact so that the length of axle doesn't shift more to one side or the other. Once the cone is loosened, the ball bearings will begin to fall out. Make sure they don't get away from you. After you've taken great care to collect them all, count them. Half that number goes to one side, half to the other. Now throw them away and use the new bearings that you've gotten.

Completely clean all the parts: cones, keyed washer, locknut, axle, quick-releases; and reassemble.

For the rear wheel you'll have to remove the freewheel first. You'll need a freewheel remover. Each manufacturer of freewheels has its own design and, consequently, a different remover.

Determine who makes your freewheel and get a remover for it.

Some are expensive and others not, but you'll need it again if you ever have to replace a spoke on the freewheel side of the hub. Remember, when you use your remover, be sure to secure it to the freewheel with your quick-release (if yours is set up with one) or with the axle nut. I've seen more people ruin their freewheels because the tool slipped off the freewheel body, stripping the notch.

After you've secured the remover properly, clamp the tool in a bench vise. Give the wheel a good twist to break the grip, then back off on the nut, retaining the remover, and loosen the freewheel some more. After doing this one or two more times, take the remover off completely and just spin the freewheel off. When you replace the freewheel later, spin it onto the hub finger tightly; the first time you ride the bike, it will tighten automatically. Caution: don't cross thread the freewheel onto the hub. If it's an alloy hub, the material is very soft, and usually this will mean a new hub and the work of relacing.

Basic Adjustments

By now, you should have most of your equipment back on the bike. Now we'll deal with the adjustments of brakes, derailleurs and the minor truing of wheels.

Adjusting the brakes is really quite simple, but the adjustment depends on how true your wheels are. In order to set your brake blocks about ⅛ inch from the rim requires that the wheels be no more than 1/16 inch plus or minus out of true.

"So what," you say, "I'll just set the brakes with more clearance." Remember that as with the brakes on a car, the closer the brakes are set, the shorter the time between seeing something and actually hitting the brakes and stopping.

If you don't have a truing stand, use the brakes as a guide for minor truing of the wheels. Set the adjusting barrel for centerpulls (on either the brake levers or on the quick-releases) all the way down, then pull the yoke cable clip up as far as possible on the brake cable, then tighten. With the clearance at a minimum, spin the front wheel and see if the wheel hangs up on either side. You can tell which way the wheel is out of true by sighting from one edge of the rim to the opposite side to see where the line of sight intercepts the hub. Then do the same on the other edge of the rim; the eye is surprisingly accurate for this degree of truing.

Use a spoke wrench to get the wheels true. Don't use a crescent wrench or you'll round off the nipple. Start by selecting one of the high spots and tighten the spoke or spokes at this point on the *low* side, half a turn at a time. Then loosen the spoke or spokes on the *high* side half a turn at a time to equalize the tension on both sides of the rim.

If the wheels of your bike are fairly old and there are signs of corrosion on the spokes, grip the spoke directly next to the nipple with a pair of Vise-Grips to prevent the spoke from twisting when you turn the nipple. Some wheel builders do this even when building with new spokes that don't have a frozen nipple problem, in order to neutralize any unwanted tension in the spoke itself. Others use the method of giving the nipple a half turn more than required, then backing off to unwind the twist in the spoke. Unless your wheel is fairly new, I would recommend the former method. It will cut down on broken spokes.

Photo 19: It is a good idea to grip the spoke with a pair of Vise-Grip pliers to keep the spoke from twisting when you tighten or loosen the nipple.

The rear wheel has to be dished to one side to accommodate the freewheel cluster. Begin by making sure that the wheel is installed in the dropout properly. Extend an imaginary line down the seatstay and through the dropout. This is where the axle should be positioned. Don't set your wheel forward, in an attempt to shorten your wheelbase. I've also seen some people jam the derailleur into the spokes and if the wheel is set forward, it can be torn out of the dropout. If this happens, the dropout might be deformed. After bending it back into shape, its strength is questionable. Now use the same technique for truing the rear wheel as you used for the front.

The best way is to use a truing stand and a dishing tool. At one time the cost of a truing stand was prohibitively expensive so that it wasn't worth the cost if it were only to be used occasionally. There is one stand, the Buzzi, distributed by Cinelli, selling for approximately $35 which I have used and found totally adequate for occasional use. Although my favorite is the VAR setup, which is a permanently bench-mounted unit, I like the portability of the Buzzi. I've designed a simple portable stand for the Buzzi so it can be knocked down for easy storage, portability and places where a bench vise (that's where the stand was designed to be used) is not available.

Once the wheels are trued, check the brake adjustment again for block to rim clearance and for centering on the rim itself. Be sure the brake block is facing in the right direction so that it doesn't slip out of the shoe under braking pressures; the open end of the shoe faces the rear.

Now check the chain. I assume that you've soaked and cleaned it by this time. Usually I soak the chain in kerosene, brush out the links, soak again, dry it and then check it for wear. It's an easy procedure. Lay the chain on its side and count off 24 links. Measure these 24 links with a 12-inch ruler from pin to pin. If they measure more than 12⅛ inches, replace the chain as it has stretched too much. The teeth on the gears where the chain contacts are not all sharing the pull exerted in pedaling equally. What happens is that wear on the chainrings and freewheel teeth accelerates; it's a lot cheaper to replace the chain periodically than to replace the chainrings and freewheel.

If you replace your chain, and then experience some skipping when you pedal, replace your freewheel, too. It has worn down to the point where it matches your old chain links, and there's no way you'll be able to make this new combination work.

If the chain has not worn appreciably, soak it in some 90-weight automotive transmission fluid. Wipe off the excess and install the chain back on the bike, using your chain rivet tool. Watch out for the stiff link.

Derailleur adjustment actually amounts to just two adjustments after the cable is anchored, but this is exactly where most people make it complicated. First, after making sure that the derailleur is firmly secured to the dropout and *without* fixing the cable, adjust the high-gear stop screw until the tension and jockey wheels are in line with the small cog of the freewheel. Now adjust the cable by setting the rear-gear lever all the way forward against the stop. (I'm assuming that you've fastened the levers, guides and housing stops in position.) Then pull the cable tight through the rear derailleur clamp and fasten it. The cable will always have just a slight amount of play after you've done this, but you can take it out by backing off on the high-gear stop screw a little. This will take out the play in the cable and insure a positive shift onto the small freewheel cog by actually overshifting the chain just enough to drop the chain into that gear.

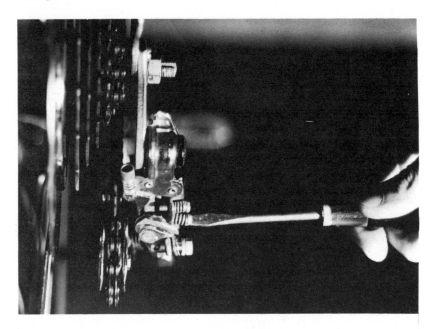

Photo 20: With the cable still off, adjust the high gear stop.

Now shift the chain up onto the large cog and line up the tension and jockey wheels with the cog, using the gear lever. Screw in the stop screw until it bottoms against the stop. Back off just a slight bit so the derailleur again overshifts to make the chain climb onto this gear. You'll have to experiment a bit with this adjustment to see how much overshift you'll need. It depends on how worn the derailleur, chain and freewheel are. Those more worn will require more overshift than a newer and tighter assembly. Needless to say, the derailleur itself should be checked, cleaned and adjusted. Be very careful not to put too much overshift or offset, because that derailleur cage or chain can and will entangle itself in the spokes and ruin the wheel.

The front derailleur should be mounted so that the cage clears

Photo 21: Maintain a ¼-inch clearance between the front derailleur cage and large chainwheel.

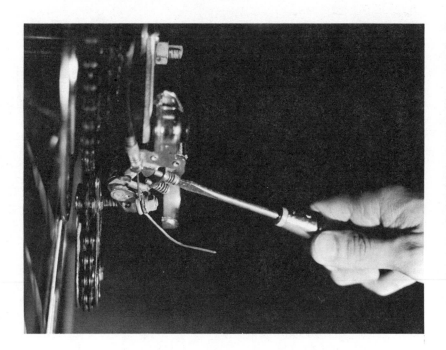

Photo 22: Adjust the low gear stop after the cable is attached.

31

the tips of the teeth on the large chainring by ¹/₁₆ to ¼ inch and should parallel both the circumference and face of the chainring. The action of the shifting lever for the front might be opposite to the rear depending upon who makes your derailleur, but the stop adjustments are the same and done identically to the rear derailleur. One word of caution: be careful of the amount of overshift you put into the large chainwheel. Too much overshift and the chain might unship on an upshift and become lodged between the crankarm and chainwheel. It can sometimes get jammed rather tightly and is a major job to separate. Put in just enough overshift and no more.

Saddle Adjustment

With all the major mechanical work finished, the only thing left to do before the bike is ridable again is to make final adjustments.

One of the most common mistakes that I see on the road is the misadjustment of saddle height. This not only makes the rider look awkward, but also doesn't let the rider exact the full potential of the energies spent in pedaling.

The formula most people use today to determine saddle height—and it's been scientifically tested—is the measurement of your inseam length, standing barefoot, times 109 percent. This gives you the correct distance between pedal and saddle top, and works out quite accurately for most people. I've used it and found that ½ inch below this measurement gives me the most comfortable riding position for my build.

If you find after working this out for yourself that it's quite a difference in height from what you've been using, don't move that seatpost up all at once. Try increasing the extension in small increments and live with them a week at a time until you reach that 109 percent mark. Once there, you'll have a fairly good idea of how comfortable that position is after a week of riding. If need be, adjust it ¼ inch one way or the other until you find what suits you best.

Many people have asked me about the position of the saddle in relation to the seatpost as they notice that mine is pushed forward a bit on one of my machines. The rule of thumb is that the extension of the centerline of the seatpost should intersect about midway on the length of the saddle. Moving the saddle ½ to 1 inch forward or backward is permissible to gain the correct pedaling position. Incidentally, I have the saddle about ¾ inch forward on my bike to position myself farther over the pedals for sprinting, but I do this for

33

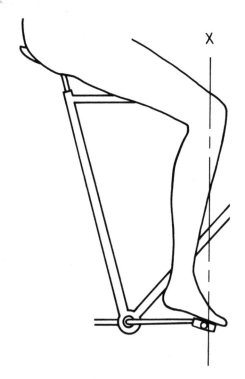

Figure 3: With the pedals at 3 and 9 o'clock, the knee joint should be directly above the pedal spindle.

a specific reason, and it's not for general riding. For touring, the position in figure 3 should be followed.

The saddle should also tilt slightly up at the nose so that your weight is automatically resting on the middle to rear of the saddle. Again, not everyone is the same, as evidenced by my saddles being level or tilted down just very slightly. Try the slight upward tilt and if it isn't comfortable, try tilting the nose up or down a slight amount and try again.

Stem length is very important as this is the deciding factor in how you distribute your weight on the bike. Too short a stem extension will give you a faster reaction at the front wheel, but your weight will be deposited mostly on your bottom. Too long a stem will put too much of your weight on your arms and hands. This position tends to aggravate the numbing of the hands and causes arm, shoulder and neck aches. The happy compromise is equal distribution of weight on your arms and bottom. I, and everyone I've ridden with, use the elbow-to-fingertip method for determining the correct length of extension. Simply place your elbow against the nose of the saddle and extend your arm toward the handlebar. Your fingertips should just touch the handlebars. Plus or minus ¼ inch is not too bad and sometimes can be taken up in the adjustment of the saddle, but anything over that will require changing to a stem with the correct extension length. Some people use an adjustable stem to facilitate things if a particular machine is used by more than one person. When installing the stem into the fork tube, make sure that you have at least 2 inches of the stem inserted, or you might end up with a broken stem. Also make sure the top of the stem is no higher than the height of the saddle.

The position of the handlebar is one of personal choice, but I would suggest that the hooks be adjusted so that they are slightly off horizontal, as shown in figure 4. For touring it's better to have the top of the hooks horizontal in order to have a more comfortable position in the saddle. Almost all racers set the bottom of the hooks horizontally so it's more comfortable to grip them when it's out-of-the-saddle sprinting time. Whichever position you prefer, be sure to position your brake levers so that it's easy to grab both of them.

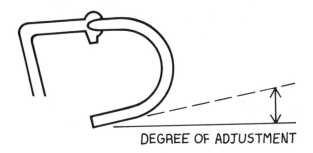

DEGREE OF ADJUSTMENT

Figure 4: The "hooks" of the handlebar are adjusted so that they are slightly off horizontal.

Many people are still adamantly against toe clips and straps because, "I won't be able to get my foot out in time." I've never seen anyone not able to extract his/her foot from a toe-clipped pedal when he/she has to. But you do have to remember certain basic rules when riding in traffic or when you anticipate stopping unexpectedly. I always loosen my straps as soon as I hit the city limits going to and from work.

To get the clips and straps to work for you, they must be fitted properly. Ideally, the ball of the foot should be located directly over the pedal axle or just slightly ahead of it. The toe clip should be sized with this fitting in mind. With the infinite sizes of feet and, correspondingly, shoes, and with only three sizes of toe clips, there's bound to be problems. There's only about a ½ inch difference in the length of each graduating size in toe clips.

Normally, a larger toe clip is all right because there should be a slight bit of clearance between the shoe and clip to keep from chafing the toes, but if you're just between sizes, a spacer of flat washers or a nut between the pedal and toe clip will solve your problem.

In selecting a set of toe straps, try to get a pair that has the least amount of stretch or give. Most on the market do stretch a bit, but if you're riding with street shoes or sneakers, they'll do. You won't be able to pull back on the back stroke without cleats. If you are using cycling shoes with cleats, get a good pair of straps that have little give so that your shoe won't come out when you don't want it to.

One thing that I do which I feel helps, especially at the time of the year when it gets dark early, is to double the end of the strap after I've inserted it through the buckle and tape around the doubled end with some reflectorized tape. This keeps the strap from accidentally coming undone, and it gives me a place to get hold of to tighten the strap, particularly when I'm wearing thick gloves or mittens. It's also a moving reflector for auto drivers to see after the sun has gone down.

Part Two
Lightening the Bicycle

Converting to Tubular Tires

How would you like to cut a few pounds off your bike? In this section I'll be discussing the replacement of certain components with lighter ones and how to set them up.

Before you even think about whether or not you want to start spending some money for lighter alloy parts, you must decide whether or not the basic frame is worth spending the extra money on. I certainly would not want to spend a lot of money on a frame that would not give me the performance I was seeking, even with the addition of some expensive parts. But on the other hand, a few good parts might make all the difference in the world, and they can possibly be used on your next machine, too. This will be the hardest part of this project, and you must give it careful consideration.

The one step that will really make the biggest difference as far as chopping off pounds is concerned is converting from clinchers to tubular or sew-up tires and wheels. This conversion not only cuts off weight but should help increase performance. The bike will accelerate faster because of the decrease in the mass of the wheels, and the handling will be much quicker because the gyroscopic effect is lessened, again because of the smaller mass at the outer circumference of the wheel assembly.

Take the extreme example: the weight of an all-steel assembly with steel hubs, solid axles, heavy gauge spokes, steel clincher rims and rubber tires weighing between 5 and 6 pounds can be quite a lot. Compare it to a typical sew-up assembly of alloy high-flange hubs, double-butted spokes, alloy road rims and 8- to 10-ounce tires, an assembly of 3½ to 4½ pounds. The latter combination is preferable if maximum paring of pounds is what you're after.

For specialized competition events even more weight can be

saved with such specialty items as the ultralight Hi-E hubs, surgically reworked Campagnolo low-flange hubs with 32 or less drillings, lighter gauge, double-butted spokes, unferruled sprint rims, the new nine-ounce rims that were made popular by Eddy Merckx on the machine used in his record one-hour ride in Mexico, and six-ounce tires; but these are delicate assemblies and not really meant for road use. Costs for specialty assemblies like these will be $100 and up, even if you do the building yourself. Even with the normal road assemblies, costs can be $75 and higher, depending on the make of parts that you use.

The majority of bikes worth spending a little money on come already equipped with alloy hubs and rims but are shod with incredibly heavy tires.

There's a compromise here that won't cost an arm and a leg but will shave nearly a pound off your existing wheels. Clement and General both make a thin and light, 10- to 11-ounce clincher tire, and when you compare this to some of the heavy, 16-ounce-plus tires, you'll find you have almost a 50 percent saving in weight. Of course, these lighter tires won't take as much abuse as the heavier ones, but neither will sew-ups. Carrying one of these as a spare is easy, because unlike the heavier clinchers, these can be looped into a small eight- to nine-inch circle. They are worthwhile looking into.

The newer, high-pressure 700 C tire and rim assemblies are also lighter than the standard from the factory assemblies but would require lacing up new rims. A distinct advantage of some of the 90 to 100 psi tires over the American standard 1¼ x 27-inch assemblies is the lower rolling resistance. Of course, there's even less with the lighter tubular setups.

If you've decided to take the plunge and go all the way with tubulars and you will build them yourself, get yourself a publication which tells you how to lace wheels. There are plenty of good magazine articles that have gone into this skill in detail, so I'll not get into it here. I will, however, give you a couple pointers which will make things easier, especially for the beginner.

When you initially thread the nipples onto the spokes, make sure that each nipple is threaded on the same number of turns, even if the spokes are still loose in the rim. This will help to insure that even tension will be achieved. It also helps minimize the initial out-of-round and out-of-true problems.

As you begin to lace the rear wheel, you'll scratch your head and ask, "I know this has to be dished to accommodate the freewheel, but how much?" If you are working on your first wheel, and don't have a dishing gauge to determine the correct angle for you, this can be a perplexing problem. The question can be solved if you think about it for a minute.

Essentially, the rim must rotate midway between the rear dropouts; therefore, measure the width between the dropouts. This is the dimension that you must have from face of axle locknut to face of axle locknut on the hub assembly. If you don't have this dimension, make width adjustments by adding or subtracting washers or thin shims until you do have it. Now measure the width of the rim, divide that dimension in half and subtract it from one-half of the dimension between the dropouts. With a marking pen mark this dimension on the hub, measuring from the face of either locknut. This is where the edge of the rim (the edge of the rim on the side of the hub you took your measurement from) should line up when you sight across the diameter of the rim as you slowly rotate the wheel. Do this periodically as you begin to increase the tension on the spokes, and you can correct the small deflections as you go along. Don't let the deflection get wild, as then you'll begin all over again.

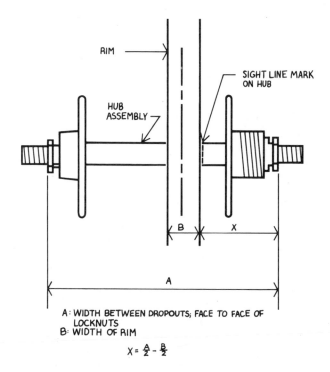

RIM

SIGHT LINE MARK ON HUB

HUB ASSEMBLY

B X

A

A: WIDTH BETWEEN DROPOUTS; FACE TO FACE OF LOCKNUTS
B: WIDTH OF RIM

$$X = \frac{A}{2} - \frac{B}{2}$$

Figure 5: Determining whether the rear wheel is dished sufficiently for the freewheel.

Of course, you can avoid all this work if you have a dishing tool, but if you lace only two pairs of wheels a year at the most and don't like to invest a lot of money in a tool that just sits on the tool rack the majority of the time, then use this method (see my previous comments on the most inexpensive truing stand I've worked with). After you're finished, the marking pen ink can be removed from the hub with a little kerosene.

A common oversight with novice wheel builders is that they forget to actually lace the outside spoke. This spoke should cross each spoke on the outside except the last one. You should lace the spoke *behind* the last crossed spoke to increase the lateral resistance of the wheel and to distribute the driving forces to a larger number of spokes.

Just for a point of reference, everything I discuss will be done to a bike which I feel is fairly representative of midrange-price machines today. This bike weighed 27 pounds as it came stock, and everything on it was steel except for the handlebars. The frame is constructed of Reynolds 531 straight-gauge on the main tubes.

Replacing the Crankset

I would like to reiterate what I said in the preceding section regarding spending the money for expensive alloy equipment. Remember, a heavy 30-pound bike will still be a heavy 27-pound bike. The difference in effort required to propel each bike differs little on the level once the bike is moving. If weight can be saved in the revolving parts, that's where the difference will count in the long pull.

Have you ever taken the steel crank assembly off your bike? Probably the first time you did you were quite surprised at how much it weighed. I know I was.

The weight savings in replacing a steel crank assembly with an alloy one will amount to about 1 to 1½ pounds. This isn't too much statistically, but dynamically, when you're spinning, there'll be a difference.

There are many alloy cranksets on the market today, and they vary in quality as well as price. The Super Record Campagnolo cranksets with the abbreviated chainrings and titanium crank spindle will cost 40 percent more than the Nuovo Record, or about $125 to $150. That's the top, so you can see what you might spend before the upper limit is reached. There are also many sets from Japan and France that are quite good, and they don't cost as much. The Sugino Mighty Competition sets can be found for about $60 if you do some shopping. Remember, you do pay for what you get, and if you're starting competition, by all means get the best you can afford. If you're not going to use it for competition, the less expensive makes will be adequate.

When you do your shopping, consider beforehand exactly what you want, and don't settle for less. There are more variations and choices for crank lengths and chainring sizes than are available with steel sets.

Most bikes come equipped with crank lengths of 170 mm or 6¾ inches. This is about as long as most average-build people would want to go and still be able to spin. If you have longer legs, you might want to try longer cranks. They'll give you more leverage, but you do have to put up with rotating through a larger circle and using more energy in moving the legs. Shorter ones will spin great but won't provide the leverage on climbs of tall gears.

Once you've determined the crank length, decide on the pedals you want to use. It's not difficult because there are only two choices: French or non-French. Everybody uses ⁹/₁₆ x 20-inch threads on their pedals, except the French. Theirs are just different enough to make them incompatible with the ⁹/₁₆ x 20-inch threads. They will sometimes work with some sloppy non-French threaded cranks, but you'll be taking a chance of stripping out the threads. The unfortunate point in this case is that many of the cheapest reliable pedals are made by the French. Thus it is difficult, if not impossible, to switch over to a better quality pedal at a later date.

In the last few years a number of economical Japanese pedals (which have English threads) have appeared on the market. This widens the choice somewhat.

The difference in the size of the chainwheel, if at all possible, shouldn't exceed 10 teeth. I know some people won't agree, but I've found that for fast, efficient changes from the small chainring to the large one, a 10-tooth difference is the limit. Of course, for general riding and touring where fast changes are not as critical, wider ranges are available and are recommended. If you're really going to be hauling around some weight for extended tours, you might consider a smaller large chainring, because with an extra 50 pounds of baggage you'll need lumberjack legs to push a 90-inch-plus gear.

Crank spindles or axles come in three different sizes: 68 mm, 70 mm and 74 mm. These are all keyed to the width of the bottom bracket. No one country makes an exclusive practice of using just one size, so you can't tell what size you have by the country of origin of your bike or present crankset. You'll simply have to measure the width of the bracket shell. If you don't have a tape or ruler with metric increments, get one. You'll need it if you plan to do much work on bikes. Almost all the countries outside the United States and Great Britain are on the metric standard. The United States is supposed to change but has been pushing the date back every few years.

The last decision you must make is what type of thread is in the bottom bracket shell itself. Then you can get the right bearing cups for it. The country of origin will generally give you a good idea of the type of threads. There are British, French and Italian threads. Japan uses British threads. It's always a good idea to double-check by bringing the adjustable cup and lockring of your present crankset to the bike shop for an actual match.

When you purchase your crankset, be sure to buy the crank tools at the same time. You'll need them. These will include the crank remover, spindle nut wrench or socket, chainring bolt hex wrench and chainring rear-fixing bolt wrench. If you have a socket that will fit the spindle bolt and a metric allen wrench set, you can forget the crankset-factory-made ones.

You might consider the purchase of a lockring spanner and pin wrench at this time. They save time and, more importantly, your temper when you find you need three hands at one time; they leave a better looking job in the end. As with most things today, they're not cheap.

Fitting a New Chainset

In fitting a new chainset, one of the biggest problems, aside from getting the correct parts, is getting the correct chainline to insure proper alignment at all 10 or 12 ratios.

Before installing any of the new parts, make one final check to see that all parts are present and that they are the right ones for your frame. There's nothing more frustrating than finding a crank spindle too long or too short, finding that the threads on the bearing cups don't match the ones on the bottom bracket, or finding that you're unable to screw the pedals onto the crankarms after all the time and trouble you've spent carefully fitting the crankset to the bike.

Once you've disassembled your original crankset, the first thing to do is to clean out the bottom bracket. Before installing anything, measure the width of the bottom bracket shell to determine its true dimension. It might not be the same as you originally thought. This doesn't happen often, luckily, but bracket shells sometimes come from the manufacturer out of true, and a conscientious frame builder will true it up by cutting the cup bearing surfaces of the shell until they're perfectly flat and perpendicular to the centerline of the crank spindle. You might also find this on cheaper bikes whose builders chose to cut corners by using parts not manufactured to accurate tolerances. The deviation may range up to 2 mm after truing; what you thought was a 68-mm bracket because of the markings on the crank spindle, might really be a 66-mm bottom bracket. This isn't as bad as it sounds, but it does cause an alignment problem and, perhaps, a chainring-to-chainstay clearance problem.

Another problem you might encounter on the better built, hand-fitted machines is this: in some cases, the person who did the assembly machined the shoulder of the fixed cup, which bears up against the bottom bracket, to ensure a square fit. This is fine until you find that there is too much thread showing on the adjustable cup beyond the lockring because a shorter spindle has been substituted. There will be clearance problems with the chainrings and chainstay. The above example doesn't apply to our installation but serves to illustrate what could be done to compound problems.

It is not too difficult to correct the problem of a narrow bracket shell. Just take the actual measured width of your bottom bracket shell and subtract it from the width shell your spindle was made for. One-half of the resulting answer will be the thickness of a spacer you'll need to correct the misalignment of the crankset.

> Example: Width of bottom bracket of spindle = 68 mm
> Actual measure width of bottom bracket = 66 mm
> Difference = 2 mm

Take half of that dimension (1 mm), and that's the thickness of the spacer you need between the fixed cup and the bottom bracket to bring the chainrings and crank out to the correct position.

Another solution is to use a slightly longer axle, as for a triple chainwheel set.

The most important dimension on the rear hub assembly is the measurement between the face of the large cog of the freewheel and the face of the axle locknut. It should be 30 mm for a 5-speed cluster. The total width between the faces of the locknuts on the rear axle

Photo 23: Measure the width of the bottom bracket after you have removed both cups to determine the actual width.

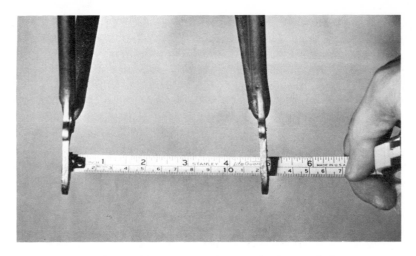

Photo 24: The width between the inside faces of the rear dropouts should be 120 mm, the same from face of locknut to face of locknut on the rear axle.

should be 120 mm. These are dimensions used by almost all frame builders today, so a quick check of your rear hub will reveal whether or not you have an odd dimension. Another measurement to check is the distance between the inside faces of the dropouts. This should also be 120 mm.

One thing I've noticed on all cranksets is that the chainrings seldom run true. They will have a variation of up to ¼ inch in some cases. This will result in the chain rubbing against the front derailleur with almost every shift. Sometimes the problem is in the chainrings and at other times in the crank pins, or both.

The way I determine the fault is by taking the chainrings individually and laying them on a flat surface to see if there's a warp in the chainring itself. If there's any runout, clamp the chainwheel in a vise (between two pieces of wood to protect the finish) and carefully bend the chainwheel in the opposite direction to straighten it up.

After straightening, fit the chainwheels onto the crank pins and check if these all line up on the same plane. Make sure that when you fit them on, you don't force them, otherwise you won't be able to tell if the crank pins are out of line or if you've swaged the chainwheels in fitting them on. Fit on both the chainwheels to see if they both give you the same reading. If you find one of the pins out of line, again clamp the crank between two pieces of wood, then wrap the offending pin with a rag and with a large crescent wrench lightly bend the pin back in line with the others. On both these operations refrain from using a heavy hand, or you're liable to bend the part too far in the opposite direction, or even fracture it.

Once you've gotten the cranks on the bike, remember that the soft alloy has a certain amount of crush to it with the initial installation. After each ride for the first 50 miles check the crank bolts to make sure that the slack caused by the seating of the cranks against the taper of the axle is taken up. If you don't, you're going to wiggle the crank on the axle with each subsequent ride, and enlarge the hole so much that you'll never be able to tighten the crank on that axle again. This holds true for the pedals, too.

I've noticed that many younger riders are leaving the dust caps off their cranksets, emulating racers. Don't. Competition riders must have quick access to the crank bolts during a race, but for any other type of riding the advantages of having the dust cap's protection far outweigh not having them. One reason: if you grease the bolts before installing them, as you should, the excess grease will pick up the dirt very easily when you're riding. If the grease is not removed and the bolt cleaned when you take it off, then upon reinstallation it could gall the threads or the soft bearing shoulder of the crank. Do this enough times and you'll have to throw away that expensive crank.

One last hint: when you install your pedals, use a thin washer between the spindle and crankarm to prevent galling the alloy crank. TA of France uses this practice and it works.

Front Derailleur Choices

There are almost as many different rear derailleurs on the market today as there are different makes of bikes. The design on the majority of these has not changed for many years. (The multi-gear derailleur was patented in 1894.) This is the swinging parallelogram design, which is excellent up to a point. The most successful use of this type derailleur is in combination with a close ratio block.

With this design the derailleur cage moves across the plane of the different gears in an arc. With the ideal setup, the arc should not progress farther than six o'clock when engaging the lowest gear, this being the bottom of the stroke. If it progresses any farther, the cage is forced to move upward, continuing on its fixed circular path. I've never seen this ideal setup on any bike.

If a wide ratio block is used with a low gear of 28 teeth or more, chances are the derailleur cage will actually hit the low gear when trying to engage it. Although the derailleur may be able to accommodate enough chain for the longer cage arm needed with wide ratio touring gears, this forced stop eliminates the derailleur from being used with a block with anything bigger than about a 28- to 30-tooth low gear, unless it's designed with the cage pivot through the jockey wheel.

Several years ago two of the most prominent Japanese bicycle component firms introduced some new derailleurs to the market and stirred up quite a commotion, in the form of a new design: the slant pantograph. This design eliminated the need for the arc to cross at right angles to the freewheel gears in the same plane as the path of the derailleur cage. Instead, with the slant pantograph the cage moves in a *straight line* diagonally across the freewheel block, keeping a more uniform distance between the jockey wheel and the

Photo 25: The swinging parallelogram derailleur moves through an arc.

gears of the freewheel all the way down to the lowest gear. This gives the pantograph a definite advantage, especially when used with the wider ratios.

Why does everything that has an advantage also have a disadvantage? Because of the offset pivoting and the longer diagonal path of the derailleur, the shift levers must be moved farther to affect a gear change, unless they're especially designed to be used with a slant pantograph. Those that are, compensate by giving the barrel of

51

Photo 26: The slant pantograph action takes a straight line and keeps a more uniform distance between the derailleur cage and freewheel gears.

the levers a larger diameter so the cables will have to travel a greater distance to achieve the same degree of lever movement required for the swinging parallelogram setup.

Another disadvantage is that the offset required in the mounting of the slant pantograph unit makes a larger body necessary, and thereby increases the weight slightly.

I've used many different derailleurs on the many bikes I've ridden, and I've formed some personal opinions and preferences for rear derailleurs. On competition bikes I prefer to use the better, precisely made, swinging parallelogram units because of the shorter lever movement needed to actuate the derailleur. Their lighter weight is an added bonus. My experience with the slant pantograph units on a number of road-test bikes and other machines has persuaded me to try this type of derailleur setup on the project machine I've been using for this book. Also, a most important consideration is the cost. The entire slant pantograph setup can still be had for the cost of just the rear Campagnolo Record derailleur.

Before reviewing some of the points of the installation of these units, I'd like to touch on the other half of the setup, the front derailleur. These units have not undergone many changes since their inception. Right now there are two types being sold. The less expensive ones have the derailleur cage moving in a straight path out from the body in an axis parallel to the axis of the crank spindle. This type is entirely satisfactory for cranksets where the chainring sizes do not differ by more than five or six teeth. Any more than this and the efficiency of the unit will be defeated, particularly when all the related drivetrain parts have had time to wear.

The preferable type of front derailleur is the swinging parallelogram unit, which moves in an arc following the diameter difference of the chainrings as it intercepts the diametric plane of each chainring as it shifts. The big advantage here is that the cage will help pick the chain up from the small chainring and assist it as it climbs to the big chainring. When derailling from the big ring, the cage, in dropping down closer to the smaller chainring, will guide the chain more closely and accurately.

One type of swinging parallelogram front derailleur is the Maeda Sun Tour line. However, the shifting action has been reversed on several of their models. If you're not used to it, this can be rather disconcerting. These Sun Tour units have one advantage in that it takes less effort to change to the larger chainring. All you have to do is shove the lever forward. This releases the tension on the derailleur and the resulting spring action pushes the cage outward. You don't have to do another thing except adjust the cage afterwards so it doesn't rub on the chain.

The disadvantage to this unit is that you can't achieve minimum tension throughout the derailleur system simultaneously. What does this mean? Briefly, the life of any spring is increased any time you are *not* putting tension on it. If you're not riding your bike, you should release as much tension on the springs as possible. With these Japanese units, tension is imposed on the rear derailleur cage when the tension in the front unit is at its minimum and vice versa.

I haven't had these Japanese units long enough to come up with any definitive test results. In the end, it might not make any difference anyway, but on my old Campagnolo units, I've had to

Photo 27: Here you can see the pivot points; the central one at the pin directly below the stop screws makes the cage swing in an arc that moves upward as it moves outward.

make an adjustment about once or twice a year to keep the proper tension on the chain. I've run out of positions to place the end tang of the spring, so lately it has meant removing the spring and untwisting it to give it more tension. I know there is a loss of tension over a period of time, depending on what gears you use, the amount of required chain, frequency of gear changes and how much you use the large chainwheel with the lower freewheel gears, thus increasing the tension to the maximum. Another questionable point is the life of an alloy cage as compared to the longer wearing qualities of steel. Finally, the Japanese use a cable housing to actuate the derailleur, and if you do a lot of riding, grit can get inside the housing and cause trouble.

Installing the Rear Derailleurs

The Japanese rear derailleurs are installed similarly to the swinging parallelogram derailleurs. In fact, they are compatible with Campagnolo dropouts if the right bolt is used. On incompatible dropouts, an adapter plate must be used.

Once the derailleur is fixed on the dropout, check the plane of the jockey and tension wheels for alignment with the freewheel gears. If they are misaligned, find out why and correct it. The most common malady seems to be a bent dropout ear that results from dropping the bike heavily or a crash. To correct this, clamp the entire dropout (and only the dropout) in a wood vise or a vise with wooden jaws to protect the finish, and with an 18-inch crescent wrench very slowly bend the fixing ear back into place. It shouldn't need much adjustment. If it does, then it's bent badly and by bending it back you'll probably weaken it more, making its strength for further use questionable. Heating the piece with a torch and bending it back can sometimes save the offending part, but this is a last resort. Normally, if you have to go this far, you'd probably be further ahead by simply replacing the dropout. If you decide to try this, find yourself someone who knows what he/she's doing.

Another trick is simply to cut off the ear if it's fastened and can't possibly be saved, and use the accompanying adapter plate. If it's a forged dropout, the extra thickness of the plate will necessitate a longer quick-release skewer for your hub.

After you've aligned the tension and jockey wheels, the arm of the slant pantograph must be adjusted so it's parallel with the chainstay. I've found that with a bit of cheating, opening up the angle between the chainstay and derailleur arm to make the diagonal path of the cage steeper, I could accommodate a bigger low gear than the manufacturer's suggested limit.

Photo 28: The manufacturer recommends the derailleur arm be adjusted parallel to the chainstay, but with a bit of cheating, a larger low gear can be used.

One complaint I have about these units is that I can't easily take them apart because they are assembled with rivets and pins. I think that quite a bit of weight could be saved by judicious paring of material. There seems to be an overabundance resulting from the casting process and not being cleaned well.

If you do decide to use one of these setups, buy the original cables for it as these are bigger in diameter than most cables and less prone to stretching. They aren't constructed as well as the Campagnolo cables with the double weave in two directions, but they're a good compromise.

The front derailleur is easier to install than the rear one because there's no alignment problem that can't be solved with the derailleur itself, unless the chainrings are out of true.

On the reversed action Japanese front derailleurs, be sure that the chain is on the big chainwheel before installing the derailleur, otherwise you won't be able to measure the required clearance between the cage and the large chainwheel. This is the critical dimension for positioning the derailleur vertically on the seat tube. With the other Japanese front derailleurs, the action is the same as on European-made units, and again the chain must be on the large chainwheel before installing. Here we must adjust the derailleur cage to the large chainwheel position with the small chainwheel stop screw to facilitate the vertical positioning of the clamp.

A gap of $3/16$ to $1/4$ inch is optimum when setting up the front derailleur and should be all that's needed between the cage's front plate and the tips of the teeth on the large chainwheel. Before tightening the clamp around the seat tube, make sure that the cage is parallel to the chainwheels. Regarding the cable and stop screw adjustments, the proper adjustments of both front and rear derailleurs can be found in the Basic Adjustments section.

By this time you're probably asking, "What does this have to do with cutting weight?" Well, weight reduction on derailleurs is not going to make a big difference (a few ounces at most). But the psychological effect might make a difference to some people. If you're really after the ultimate in a production-assembly derailleur, try the Huret Jubilee, weighing about six ounces. For me, the definite shifting characteristics of the slant pantograph units with wider ratios far offset the weight reduction aspect in this case.

Seatpost Options

A popular item that more and more cyclists are using is the lighter allen-head and the S.A.E.-head seatpost binder bolts. Besides having a slight weight advantage, they also make the theft of your expensive saddle and seatpost more difficult. A word of caution on these binder bolts: they are usually not as strong as the normal nut and bolt combinations because of the reduced diameter and bearing area of the threads. Some do break or their threads strip. This is not limited to just one make either; they all do it. I used several Campagnolo models before installing the present one, but it's been on one of my machines now for two years without any signs of weakening.

I had a problem on my commuting bike with the allen-head bolt. I use centerpull brakes, and the familiar Weinmann rear cable housing hanger is attached with a binder bolt. You'll find that the majority of the allen-head bolts are too short to be used with the added thickness of the hanger, but TA makes one that is about $3/16$ inch longer than most and includes two chromed washers to space out the bolt if a centerpull hanger is not used. They also make one with a hanger included.

The S.A.E. bolt appeared on the market some years ago. This uses an S.A.E. wrench, which looks like a star with 12 points in cross section, rather than the familiar hexagonal allen wrench. This bolt seems to be stronger than most others and lighter. It comes in three lengths, so if any amenities are fastened along with this bolt, they won't present any problems.

Another minor weight saving can be achieved through the use of an alloy seatpost. The major advantage with this item is really not so much the weight differential but rather the microadjustment that can be made to obtain the optimum angle or tilt of the saddle. The difference in weight between the alloy units and a steel post with accompanying saddle clip is approximately five to six ounces, depending on which make alloy post you choose to use.

In recent years many new alloy posts have appeared on the market. All have been copies or variations of the Campagnolo design, some of them good and some not so good.

Most of the alloy posts using the Campagnolo design will weigh within one ounce of each other, so your choice will be based on quality and the price you're willing to pay. A good Japanese copy like the SR Royal will cost 25 percent less than the Campagnolo item and will weigh the same.

TTT was the first to introduce the current trend to a one-bolt, alloy post. A cross between the Campagnolo and the Simplex designs, it's a bit more complex in its workings. To conserve weight it uses only one binding bolt to secure the saddle wires. It's not as strong a design, but this model, with its fluted shaft and color-anodized finish, is 2½ ounces lighter than similar posts.

Saddles have been a sore point with many people for as long as bicycles have existed. I've known people who will go through anything to keep a saddle that they've found fitted their anatomy comfortably. Two types of saddles are normally considered by serious riders—the ever popular but heavier leather saddles and the newer, lighter, molded plastic ones.

As far as weight is concerned, the plastic ones have it. They're about half as heavy as the Brooks B17 leather ones, the standard for leather saddles for many years. The choice is a hard one, and it boils down to whether you value lightness or initial comfort. The reason I differentiate between these two qualities is that you cannot foresee how one's tender parts will react until a number of miles have been logged on the saddle. Not all dealers are understanding enough to allow customers a trial period; so it's still a buy/try situation.

Leather saddles can be treated to make them soft. They will eventually conform to your own dimensions; so comfort is almost assured after a break-in period.

A point to remember: a plastic saddle is and will be as comfortable or uncomfortable as your first time on it. A leather saddle does improve with time, reaches a peak and then begins to deteriorate. This does, however, take many years.

I use an Avocet plastic saddle on one of my bikes and a leather Brooks Professional on another machine. Both are comfortable. I tried numerous plastic models before finding the present one. Another leather one I have is an old Wright saddle of the swallow design with the side flaps cut off. It's been through a lot, but I wouldn't part with it for a dozen plastic ones. One other thing: the vinyl saddles will not take as much punishment as the leather ones.

Lightweight Pedals and Pumps

I've used Japanese pedals on and off for a couple of years, and they're not bad, but they're far from being inexpensive. Currently available is an alloy cage model, and it seems to work quite well. However, the alloy used has a lower tensile strength than some, so a thicker-walled cage is necessary. The extra material doesn't increase the weight too much, but it doesn't fit the old cleats or shoeplates. European cleats are made with narrow slots to accommodate thinner-walled pedal cages, and these cleats will have to be filed out to make them compatible with the thicker Japanese pedals. The KKT alloy cages are the same thickness as the European pedals.

A comparatively new item that's hit the market is the Non-Pedal by Cinelli. I haven't tried these yet, but they are supposed to be lighter than conventional ones because the cage is eliminated from the pedal altogether. The cost is expected to be nearly double that of the best pedals available today.

Speaking of pedals, there are currently available some aluminum alloy toe clips. These are just a bit lighter than the chromed spring-steel ones. They do have a disadvantage. There's no spring action, and if the tongue becomes squashed, it stays squashed and you can't insert your foot into the clip. Other than that, it's a good clip. Galli has come out with a titanium clip, but the price may be too expensive for some people.

Pumps are varied, and they usually don't receive the consideration they deserve until they're needed, and then it's too late. Have you ever tried putting 80 pounds of air in a tire with a hand pump? Many pumps aren't capable of inflating this high. There are a few pumps in the $10 range that will do the job properly and are worth mounting on the frame.

Basically, there are two types, the plastic models and the metal ones. I've found the aluminum ones like the Zefal (seven ounces) to be the most durable over the long haul. Such plastic ones as the Silca (five ounces) will become brittle and crack after a period of exposure to the weather. They do, however, have the advantage of being lighter in weight and are produced in just about any color to match the frame. And they are immune from dents which sometimes render the metal pumps inoperative.

I always check the diameter of the pump body and its length since the rate the air enters the tire is directly related to these dimensions. If you're a small person and not muscular, then a smaller-sized pump might be the answer, as each stroke will take less effort, but it will require more strokes to achieve the same inflation.

Stems are one area where you should not compromise lightness for strength. Most of the better models will weigh about 8½ ounces, depending on the size extension. There are other alloy stems that will weigh up to 12 ounces, and steel ones weigh even more.

Currently there are two types of binders used in stems: a conical expander plug and a truncated wedge. The conical plug is preferable to the wedge as the wedge concentrates more pressure laterally in only two directions, and it doesn't take much to split the steering tube. Generally the wedge will weigh more than the plug.

Alloy handlebars of various manufacturers do not vary much in weight. The only weight savings you might find would be in switching from a steel one to an alloy one.

Most makers produce about three different road model handlebars whose only difference is the amount of drop of the hooks. Bars should be selected with both the rider's build and riding style in mind. The rider with longer arms and torso should use a deeper drop in order to achieve a lower frontal profile. However, this rule doesn't apply at all times. The one variable is whether you will feel comfortable in a position. Some people have to grow into a position, and other people achieve the same end with shallow bends and more bend at the elbows. Try simulating different bars by inserting your stem into the steering tube to different points and then decide. Remember, always have at least two inches of the stem inserted into the steering tube.

One of the smaller things that most people tend to overlook is the use of alloy washers, spacers and fasteners. These can be used in many different places, one of the most common being the brakes. Alloy shoes can be exchanged for steel ones, alloy washers can be exchanged for steel ones, nuts for the brake shoes can be made of alloy, but not the nut that retains the whole assembly on the frame—

this one takes too much stress and is best made of stronger steel. On the whole, it's best to leave the highly stressed connections in steel. The ideal is to replace all the steel fasteners with high-tensile alloy aircraft nuts and bolts, but that's an expensive proposition, and I don't know of very many retail outlets that extensively stock this line.

Photo 29: The Sun Tour Winner aluminum alloy-cogged freewheel gives about 40 percent reduction of weight compared to steel ones of equal quality.

One of the newest items to hit the bike scene is the alloy freewheel. About two to three years ago Everest introduced their titanium freewheel. Last year Regina came out with their new model. Prior to that aluminum alloy freewheels were the lightest weight units. About the only manufacturer still making the aluminum cogged freewheels now is Zeus. On the average, these clusters will save about 40 percent off the steel counterpart of the same size.

The biggest detriment to these units is the price: $55 to $75 for the aluminum alloy models and $90 and up for the titanium unit. Unless you're racing and need to eliminate that last gram, it's not worth it.

Incidentally, Everest also makes a titanium chain, half the weight of a steel chain.

The Lightened Bike in Review

I started out with a 28-pound project bike and have been following the same steps as I've described here to lighten it. Now let's see whether it was worth the effort.

The very first thing I did was to build up a set of sew-up wheels, and this made the most significant difference of any one operation. The problem was that once I felt the difference the new wheels made, I wanted to keep making other changes. It's much like eating peanuts—once you start you can't stop until you're completely finished.

The old steel chainset got swapped for an alloy set with chainwheels more suited to my type of riding. This killed two birds with one stone, as I've been wanting to change the chainwheels for quite awhile. I didn't change the freewheel, but I did save a few grams by using some smaller and higher ratio cogs.

The old steel rattrap pedals were replaced with some lighter steel platform ones from France. The new ones work very well for me as I use this bike for commuting, and the platform pedals don't have the upturned cage at the end. I can wear my street shoes to work and still be able to get them on the pedals and into the toe straps. (I would have used alloy track pedals, which are also flat, but the cost would've gone out of sight.)

I installed a new SR alloy seatpost but have since removed it in order to work it over to see if any excess material can be removed to lighten it further. As I reported earlier, this seatpost weighs the same as the Campagnolo one but has a much greater wall thickness and more material at the clamp and seat for the saddle frame wires to make up for the weaker alloy that's used. I think perhaps two to three ounces can be removed by cleaning up around the clamp area and either fluting the outside of the shaft or reaming out the inside diameter a millimeter or two. The total weight reduction from the original bike was 2½ pounds, plus or minus a few ounces. It doesn't really sound like much, but it's almost 10 percent of the original weight. If you live and cycle on relatively flat terrain, I would say no, it's not worth the expenditure to cut the weight down by such a small amount. However, if you're living and riding in very hilly country, it could be worth it. Analyze the riding that you do and count the total vertical distance you have to climb on a typical ride. This will tell you how much extra weight you have to carry. Using this bike for commuting, I climb approximately 1,000 vertical feet every day. That's like carrying an extra 2½ pounds on your back and climbing a 1,000-foot mountain. This is not an accurate comparison, as the horizontal vector, wind resistance or advantage, and friction losses have not been accounted for, but it does demonstrate what I'm trying to explain. Basically, if you do a lot of riding in hilly or mountainous areas, you do pay for carrying any extra weight.

On fairly flat terrain, extra weight will be felt the most when you're accelerating or decelerating. Once in motion the energy expended to keep the bike at a constant velocity is virtually unnoticeable as compared to a slightly lighter machine. If you ride in an urban or heavy-traffic area, try to pick the routes where you will encounter the least amount of cross traffic and stop-and-go situations where you're constantly accelerating and braking, and you'll save on energy.

Back to the subject of wheels, at the risk of repeating myself. This one change does make the biggest difference in the overall picture. It not only reduces the static, or plain old deadweight, but it also reduces the dynamic weight, which is the weight of the wheels once they are in motion.

Should you try to lighten your bike? In my case, the deciding factor was cost. For the project bike the total price of the parts alone amounted to $135, not to mention the many hours in fitting and adjusting these parts on the bike. Timewise, it took me 10 to 12 hours to make the changeovers without any special tools. For someone not familiar with a bike, it'll take longer. For someone who has worked on bikes before and has the proper, special tools, it would take perhaps 6 to 7 hours, including the lacing of the wheels.

It's an expensive process, and as I said in the beginning, make sure in your own mind that it's worth the cost, both from the standpoint of whether the basic frame is worth it and if your pocketbook can stand it.

Part Three
Basic Repairs and Adjustments

Repairing a Broken Stem

The cardinal rule to prevent stem breakage is: insert your stem into the fork tube at least two inches. Sometimes you have to go deeper, depending on how much of the fork tube is threaded. Try to avoid expanding the end of the stem into the threaded portion of the fork tube. This is the weakest part of the tube because the metal has been removed in the threading process, making it thinner than the unthreaded portion. It becomes expensive to replace the fork, let alone the stem. But if you've been lucky enough (or unlucky enough) to have broken just the expansion part of your alloy stem, there's still a chance to make it usable again.

The first thing to do is to remove the bolt and expander plug from the stem. Next, cut off the broken part of the stem directly above the fracture. If you're using a bench vise, be sure to wrap the stem up well before clamping the vise, otherwise the jaws of the vise will dig into the soft alloy metal, ruining the stem.

The next operation can either be done with a coarse rat-tail file or a coarse tapered grinding stone and a ¼-inch drill. I personally prefer to use the file because the soft alloy of the stem fills the cavities of the grinding stone in no time at all, making it unusable. Take the file and file a tapered edge inside the end of the stem, working slowly (see figure 6). Use the shape of the expander plug to guide the amount of taper and how much metal has to be removed from the stem. You've removed enough metal when you can start the plug about ⅛ inch into the stem. After this step, wrap some fine emery cloth around your rat-tail file and clean the rough spots on the inside taper and around the edges. Next, take a hacksaw and saw a one-inch-deep slot in the end of the stem parallel with the stem sides. This is so the plug can force the stem against the fork tube when the expander bolt is tightened, and the plug is drawn into the stem. The last step is to drill a ⅛-inch hole at the top of the slot. This will relieve some of the stress when you tighten the expander bolt and prevent fractures from starting at that point.

All you've got to do now is to install the stem back on the bike. Remember, don't overtighten the expander bolt or you'll break the end of the stem again. Tighten just enough so you can't twist the stem inside the fork tube; forget that one extra turn of the bolt for good luck.

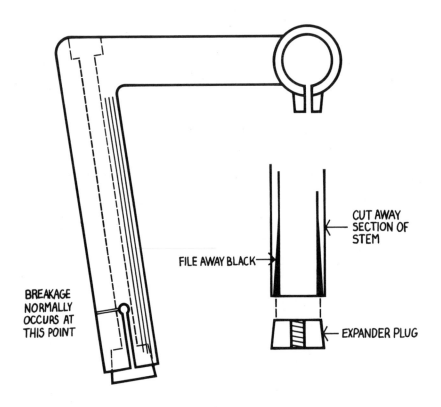

BREAKAGE NORMALLY OCCURS AT THIS POINT

FILE AWAY BLACK

CUT AWAY SECTION OF STEM

EXPANDER PLUG

Figure 6: Filing a tapered edge inside the end of the broken stem.

I don't know of any hard and fast rule for the adjustment of the stem height. Each person is made differently, so each will have a different comfortable riding position. The only thing you should not do is extend the stem any higher than the height of the saddle. I normally have my stem about one to two inches below my saddle—this distributes my weight equally between my arms and my seat, which is what you should be trying to achieve.

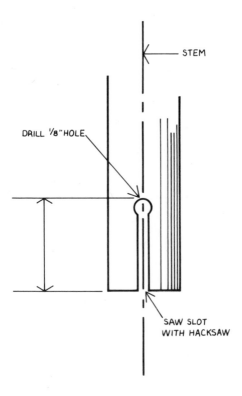

STEM

DRILL ⅛" HOLE

SAW SLOT
WITH HACKSAW

Figure 7: To relieve some of the stress on the stem, drill a ⅛-inch hole at the top of the slot.

Wrapping and Padding the Handlebars

How many times have you gone to retape your handlebars and bought a couple of rolls of cloth tape, only to find that you ran out with only an inch of the handlebars left to cover? Then you unwrapped what you had already done and used a less overlapping pattern and finished it off with just barely enough tape left to tuck into the handlebar ends. And then you noticed all the adhesive that had stuck to the top of the tape where you had to rewrap it.

The solution to this sticky problem is a visit to your local fabric shop. In its notions department ask for twill tape. You'll want at least 20 feet to cover both handlebars with enough tape so that you won't have to skimp when you're wrapping. The tape comes in all colors and widths, but anything from ¾-inch to 1¼-inch width is best. Narrower tapes take too much tape to wrap. Wider tape will pucker when you go around the bends. The last time I bought some, it was selling for five cents a foot. One advantage I like about this tape is that when it gets dirty, you can take it off, wash it and rewrap the bar with the same tape.

If you'd like to install some padding on your handlebars to help take up the road shocks a bit, this can be accomplished in two ways. I've used both ways, and they both work well. The first is more difficult but more economical.

Get an old automobile inner tube that is no longer usable and can be cut up. Measure that distance between the portion of the flat part of the handlebars you want to cover and your brake levers. Subtract about ½ inch from that measure to allow space for the taping to begin when you start wrapping. Cut two pieces of tube (the length you've just determined and six inches wide). Cut the six-inch dimension along the trunk section of the inner tube so that the natural curve of the rubber will conform to the curve of the handlebars.

Next, get yourself a roll of plastic electrical tape to secure the rubber after you've stretched it onto the handlebars. Now comes the hard part. Take one of the pieces that you have cut out and wrap it on the handlebars between the stem and the brake levers butting up as close to the brake lever as possible. It takes some getting used to, but it can be done. At this point you might find it easier to have someone else wrap the electrical tape around the rubber to keep it from unwrapping. Make sure all the puckers in the rubber have been stretched out. Now try the bar to see if you have the amount of padding you want. Cut some off if it's too much or cut new pieces if there is not enough. I've always found six inches to be more than enough. Do the rest of the handlebar the same way and then wrap it all up with handlebar or twill tape.

The second method involves simply wrapping several layers of some inexpensive, ¾-inch cotton tape on the bar before wrapping it up with the more expensive twill tape. The important thing to remember with this method is to make sure that each layer is wrapped in the same direction as the underlying one. Then you won't have the top tape working the underlying layer loose as you pull it tight.

Repairing Frayed Cables

One of the things that plagues the average cyclist when working on his/her machine is frayed brake or derailleur cable ends. They not only make a bike look unkempt, but also are dangerous to fingers and hands, as the strands always have a tendency to scratch and puncture the skin. But most of all, a frayed cable is weak at the frayed point and invariably it will break when you're on a ride far from home, with no spare. Always carry a spare rear brake and derailleur cable on long rides.

A new cable will start fraying from the day you install it. This normally happens when you trim off the excess cable because most people don't have the proper cable cutters. These have cutting blades which are circular in shape and literally surround and sever the cable intact. Instead, the average cyclist uses a pair of diagonal wire cutters which has straight cutting blades and tends to squash and spread the strands of the cable as it is being cut. If the cable end survives this operation, it is subjected to further fraying when you start trying to poke it through cable yokes and clamps while installing the cable or adjusting the brakes and derailleurs.

You can install the little plastic cable end protectors, however. These work fine for protecting your hands and fingers, but they don't really keep the cable from fraying. You'll find also that they only fit the smaller Weinmann and Mafac cables.

The only thing I've found that keeps cables from fraying is tinning or applying solder to the cable to keep all the little strands together. It's very simple and takes only a minute to do. I have found that the best way to apply solder is to start with a new cable, although it can be done with an older cable if it isn't too badly frayed and deformed.

Measure the cable for the correct length and mark where it is to be cut. Heat the cutting area with a soldering gun (or in a pinch a match will do) and apply electrical solder until it runs freely onto the cable. Then while the cable is still hot, wad up a rag and wipe off the excess solder. Install the cable and cut off the excess where you've marked it and behold—no frayed ends. Although it isn't necessary, I normally reheat the cable after trimming and apply just enough solder to form a small ball at the very end of the cable. This does two things: one, it gets rid of the sharp end of the cable and two, it makes it more difficult for someone to steal your brakes.

Caring for the Headset

One of the most neglected items on a bike is the headset. This assembly, along with the hubs, takes all the punishment a road surface can dish out and should receive its fair share of attention. Yet in talking to people who normally take an interest in giving their machines regular maintenance, I found that they didn't look at the headset and didn't know what to do if they had to replace the races.

The headset assembly is really quite simple once you have it apart and see what it is comprised of. The installation, however, must be done carefully to insure alignment, otherwise premature failure will result.

To begin, remove the stem from the steering tube along with the bars and brake levers. This means you'll have to disconnect the brake cables from the calipers. This, I think, is what really discourages most people from ever beginning the whole operation; it seems to get quite involved from the onset.

Second, remove the locknut from the steering tube. This will require a fairly large wrench or a special spanner in the case of the Stronglight units. Be careful in loosening this nut because even if you replace the races, the nut will be used again. I've seen a careless mechanic round off one pair of flats on this nut by not tightening the wrench adjustment properly. Yes, it's still usable with two more pairs of flats, but it looks ugly.

Next, remove the spacers, lock washers and brake cable housing hanger (if you have centerpull brakes). Take the same care in removing these items as with the locknut.

Finally, unscrew the top race of the upper bearing set. When you do this, make sure the front wheel is setting on the floor or the ball bearings of the lower bearing set will all drop out when you've loosened the upper race enough for them to escape. As it is, the bearings from the top set will come rolling out as soon as you loosen the top race enough. Catch these bearings so you can count them for the proper replacement number. Now lift up on the frame and the ball bearings of the lower race will drop out.

The best way to extract the bearings is to lay the bike on its side and let the bearings drop into a container, one race at a time. If you do it this way, remember to protect the pedal assembly with a short plank or rag or it might get bent or scratched; it will also protect the floor.

Now separate the fork assembly from the frame. Inspect the bearing races carefully and see if there's any wear. Be especially critical with the lower bearing set because it's this one that takes the brunt of the road shock that's transmitted by the front wheel, and all of it if the headset is adjusted loosely. On occasions when the headset is loose and you're standing on it on a climb, or accelerating hard, the majority of your weight is on the front wheel. Adding up the area of the lower race of my headset, I have come up with just a little over ¼ square inch of bearing surface.

Multiply your body weight by four for a total force on the lower race. Then divide this figure by the number of bearings in the race, and you have the loading per square inch on each bearing. It's quite a bit. And it's even worse when you hit a pothole in the road because you have impact loading for the instant you hit, which can multiply the original force many times, depending on the speed you're traveling.

If the headset is correctly adjusted, multiply your body weight by two and divide by the total number of bearings in the entire set and you can see it drops the loading on each bearing drastically. So keep it adjusted.

Sometimes if you watch more experienced riders who are acutely aware of the increased wear resulting from hitting bumps and holes in the road, you'll find they jump or lift themselves over these obstacles while maintaining their forward speed. This will decrease the punishment on the headset and wheels, making them last a lot longer. If you attempt this maneuver, remember to use toe clips and straps.

If, after inspecting the races for wear, you find that replacement is necessary, you'll need to make a tool to drive the two races out of the head tube. I've found a simple wedge-shaped stick of hardwood such as oak is best because a metal drift, even one of brass, doesn't have the resiliency to insure that the steering tube won't be deformed or nicked when the races are driven out (see figure 8).

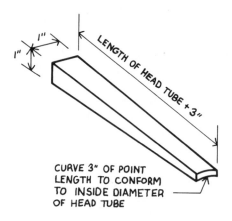

1"

1"

LENGTH OF HEAD TUBE + 3"

CURVE 3" OF POINT
LENGTH TO CONFORM
TO INSIDE DIAMETER
OF HEAD TUBE

Figure 8: To drive the races out of the head tube—when you don't have the right tool—make a wedge-shaped tool out of oak.

When you begin driving the races out, tap gently around the race. Don't bang on it and expect that a hard blow will loosen the part; it won't. Easy does it. A little patience will save your frame.

Removing the race on the steering tube is sometimes a little difficult. It should come off with a little prying with a screwdriver; but if after you've started, it still is reluctant to come off, then you can use a small wooden washer tool that you also can use to install the new race (see figure 9). Just insert it under the race with the wedge between the fork crown, then tap the end of the tool gently and move it around the steering tube as you tap, and it should loosen the race enough for it to come out.

When out, take the complete headset to your local bike shop and seek a replacement. Make sure the new headset matches the old exactly where it fits into the head tube and steering tube.

Installation takes just as much care as removal. When putting the races back on the head tube, use a flat piece of board that sits squarely on the race. Tap gently all around until the race bottoms out completely. Be especially careful of the race on the steering tube because it is the least substantial of the entire set, and it goes out of true the easiest. If the race does get bent and is not flat or concentric, then all the bearings will not receive the same loading. This will result in an uneven loading situation and accelerated wear of the headset.

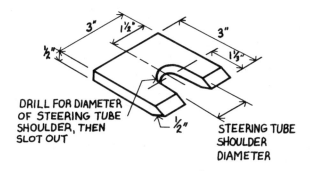

DRILL FOR DIAMETER
OF STEERING TUBE
SHOULDER, THEN
SLOT OUT

STEERING TUBE
SHOULDER
DIAMETER

Figure 9: A wooden washer tool is used to install the new races.

This race should slip on over the steering tube with the minimum amount of play and lay flat on the fork crown and perpendicular to the axis of the steering tube.

On a few bikes I've worked with, I've had to persuade the race back on with the wooden washer tool. This is used in conjunction with the wooden drift by first starting the race over the threaded portion of the steering tube and down onto the shoulder by the fork crown. Then place the wooden washer over the race and gently drive the race and washer down by tapping the drift on and around the washer with a hammer.

In replacing the ball bearings, use loose balls if your headset had or has caged bearings. You can get more bearings in the races and distribute any loads over a wider area. Simply smear the lower race in the head tube with grease, turn the frame upside down, drop the bearings into the race and insert the fork assembly. Now maintaining pressure on the race so the lower bearings don't fall out, turn the frame right side up, smear a liberal amount of grease on the upper race, screw on the upper race enough to still permit the installation of the bearings, drop them in and screw down the race just snug enough to gain the correct adjustment; slip on the washers, hangers and locknut and tighten.

Replace all of the hung-on equipment, adjust the brakes and perform a final check on the headset adjustment this way: apply the front brake and rock the bike forward and backward to see if there's any rocking that can be felt in the headset. Yes? Then tighten and try again. No? Then pick up the front of the bike and rotate the fork assembly to see if it's too tight. If so, loosen it up and try it again until it's right. Remember the loading situation I described earlier. Too tight and you dimple the races with just the tension in the adjustment; too loose and 100 percent of the loading will be imposed on the lower race.

Next time you see a hole or bump you can't avoid, think of your headset.

Overhauling the Hubs

Several weeks ago a friend of mine tried a set of wheels on his bike that were laced on a pair of popular expensive hubs and commented on the smoothness and lack of friction as compared to his own wheels. He was sold after that, but in shopping around for a pair of quality hubs he discovered that current prices made the total cost of a new pair of wheels very expensive.

In checking around, I found that there are many hubs that are not as well finished on the outside nor as well machined on the internal parts but which I feel would be quite satisfactory and comparable with the more expensive hubs after a small amount of work. Some of the less expensive ones do well with mere polishing.

The internal parts of any rotating component are the most critical as these are what dictate, for the most part, the amount of running friction. This is true not only of hubs but of other rotating equipment also, such as bottom bracket, freewheel and pedals. Therefore, the checking of all parts and final polishing of the races that I'm going to outline here are applicable to all these components as well as to hubs.

First, see if the hub, as it comes off the bike or from the box, is adjusted properly. If not, adjust the cones so there's no play, yet the axle is free to rotate without binding. Now rotate the axle with your fingers and see if there's any spot where it might be binding. If there is, you know you'll have to look for it.

Next, disassemble the hub and clean every part thoroughly. (Remember the sequence of assembly; make a sketch if you have to as you tear it down.) Now look at the cup races inside the hub shell and see if there is any uneven wear pattern or if the races are just plain worn out. If worn out, you might check with your local bike shop to see if replacements are available. More than likely, they won't be. They are not a normally stocked item with most shops. If unavailable, unfortunately, new hubs are the only answer.

If the races are not worn, or if you're working with new hubs, check to see if the axle is completely straight. Do this by rolling the axle on a completely flat surface. If it rolls readily, it's good; if not, get a new one. I've tried straightening bent axles and I've gotten very close but never perfectly true. The bend, however slight, always shows up after the axle's back on the bike.

The cones, if this is an old hub, normally receive the most wear. (The unit is designed for this—the cones are the easiest part to replace.) If there are any grooves, pits or nicks where the bearing path is, get new ones.

With the new parts you'll notice machining marks on the hub-bearing cups and cones. These are the things we want to get rid of to help reduce friction. To do this you'll need twice the number of ball bearings that go into the hubs. You'll also need some very fine automotive valve-grinding compound, which is available from any automotive supply store. Mix it with some grease for a bodied compound. You can also use a paste polish such as Simichrome. The Simichrome is better as it's much easier to handle as it comes from the tube, but it does take a bit longer to obtain the desired results because of the fineness of its abrasives.

Use the Simichrome (or grease compound) as you would regular grease, packing the hub and axle assembly. Put it all together, adjust the cones, then simply start spinning the axle. If the hub is completely laced up, spin the whole wheel by hand. Do this for about 20 to 30 minutes, then disassemble the hub and clean everything out. Inspect the cups and cones to see if you've achieved the mirrorlike finish that you want. If not, repeat the process for another 10 to 15 minutes. You might want to do this operation with an electric hand drill, but it's very easy to apply too much pressure with the drill and ruin the insides. If you do use a drill, go easy. Disassemble, clean completely, remove every trace of polish, throw the used bearings away, pack the new bearings with grease and reassemble. If you've done the polishing properly, friction will be reduced and the hub will run much smoother.

Don't be misled into thinking that if a little is good, more is better. With this process, it isn't. Too much polishing will wear a groove in the cones and cups and eventually wear through the casing, rendering the parts unusable. Do just enough to get rid of the machining marks and use just enough grease to make all the parts revolve easily.

Again, make sure you remove the last trace of polishing compound before reassembling the unit, as any residual compound will contaminate the new grease and will accelerate the wear of the internal parts.

This same process can be used for both the bottom bracket and pedals by following the same procedure. You can also use it on the freewheel, but a different procedure must be followed. The procedure for freewheels is actually a two-part process as we can polish both the bearing races and, to a certain extent, the pawl and ratchet assembly.

After first disassembling the freewheel, restrain the springs if they are not removable from the body, by either a small rubber band or some thread looped several times around the collar where the spring anchors onto the body. Apply the Simichrome to the races, insert the ball bearings and reassemble completely but without the pawls. Then start spinning. Do this and check at 15-minute intervals to see if you've gotten that nice shiny finish. Once you start to achieve this finish, put the pawls back in and apply a very light amount of Simichrome to the pawls and ratchet teeth. Don't put so much on that it will hang the pawls up and prevent contact of pawl to teeth. Put it all back together again and spin the unit. Check the ratchet often because the polishing compound will get scraped off between the teeth, and you'll have to apply more until it's loaded enough to carry from tooth to tooth while you're spinning the unit.

Once again, don't overdo it or you'll either destroy the unit or shorten the life of the freewheel.

After you've gotten the almost mirrorlike degree of polish on the races and to a lesser degree on the pawls and tips of the ratchet teeth, clean the whole thing completely and thoroughly, making sure all the polishing compound is removed including any that may have gotten on the gears. Reassemble with the new bearings and *no lubricant*. Then squirt some oil into the races after assembly.

This operation will not help all bikes because the eventual wearing of these parts will achieve the same end. It works best on a brand-new machine.

Tightening the
Stem Expander Bolt

From time to time I find that one has to review things that seem basic to people involved in bicycles every day. This was brought to focus by my son who is just getting interested in the mechanical side of bikes and is attempting to restore a vintage 26-inch-wheeled French machine. In tearing the bike down, some interesting results of poor workmanship in assembly—compounded by age—came to light.

One was the result of the strong-arm method used to tighten the stem expander bolt. No, the steering tube didn't rupture, but presumably it came close. In overtightening the bolt the expander plug had been drawn up quite a way into the stem. Our light taps on the stem bolt did not free the plug, an indication of things to come. Further blows still failed to dislodge the expander cone. Finally, we put a two-by-four under the fork crown so the force of the blows could not be absorbed by the forks, and several more hard blows did it. Even then the stem needed persuasion to come out of the steering tube.

The most frustrating part of the front end disassembly was the removal of the headset races. As I said, this was a French bike. It had the typical French headset with knurled, rounded races instead of the more workable, six-sided nut type designed for a wrench.

Normally, the race would spin right off, but because of the stem problem, the race would only back off so far, then stop as if the threads were damaged. They seemed all right, though. Closer inspection revealed that the overtightening of the stem bolt had actually bulged that part of the steering tube to the point where the race would not pass beyond it.

No amount of persuasion would budge the race. We tried using channel lock pliers, which damaged the finish of the chromed race. We even clamped the race in a vise and tried turning the fork, but to no avail.

Finally, we had to back the race down as far as possible and actually run a die on the threads, recutting them at the bulge. Even after that there was a fair amount of resistance because the die, being tapered at the starting end, did not cut down as far as the race. However, with a special pair of pliers we were able to exert enough of a grip on the round race and finally remove it.

The next time I work on a French headset I'm going to be sure the race has either a provision to use a wrench or has holes so I can use a bottom bracket lockring tool on it.

Without the correct tools, including some special ones, I don't think that I could have done this job without seriously botching up something.

My son did learn some things from this one experience: how fragile tubing is, to insert the stem past the threaded portion of the steering tube, and not to tighten the stem bolt more than necessary.

Another installation technique obvious to all "vets" but unfamiliar to my son was the required fitting of cotters on cranksets. He had replaced a cotter without fitting it to the crank axle, and this resulted in a squeak with every pedal revolution.

Remember, the cotter must be filed and fitted to each crankset. To accomplish this you must have a fine, flat file and something to hold the pin, such as a vise.

First take your new cotter pin and darken the flat side with a marking pen; then insert it into the crank. Push it in as far as it will go by hand and then give the heel a light tap with a hammer. When you take it back out, there should be marks where the cotter's surface must be filed down.

Secure the cotter in a vise and file the end with the marks on it, making sure you keep the whole surface smooth without any breaks or angle changes.

Don't take too much off before checking the fit again. Then cover the filed surface with the marking pen and begin all over. Do this until you get an even impression on the cotter, then cinch it up. Check and tighten the cotter if necessary after your first few rides, and it should be fine until the next time you change cotters.

Before preparing the frame for painting, we checked the geometry to insure that the ensuing work would not be wasted. All you need for these operations is a long piece of string and an accurate tape measure, preferably one with metric graduations.

The first check is performed on the main triangle. Begin by running the string through the bottom bracket shell, then up and around the head tube, hanging it on the lip of the down tube lug, then back down to the bottom bracket. Tie the ends together, making sure the string is taut.

Simply measure the distance from the string to the down tube on each side to check if that tube is straight. This tube is the one on the main triangle that suffers most with any head-on stack-ups. Each tube can be checked the same way, although you are only checking for the trueness of the tubes.

To check the track of the frame, run the string through the dropouts, then around the head tube and back again. The clearance from the frame to string on each side at any point including the stays should be the same. If not, then the frame isn't true and won't track straight. It should be taken to someone with the correct alignment tools and knowledge to do the job right.

Too often I have seen dinged and flattened tubes caused by people using the incorrect tools and/or methods. This is especially true with the lighter weight tubing. You can literally pinch some specialty tubes and leave a dent. A frame can only be weakened so far until it is dangerous to ride. This is one time the job should be left to the pros.

Overhauling the Freewheel

The first thing to do is to remove the cluster from the wheel. You loosen the cover plate on the freewheel body *before* taking the unit off the hub. On the majority of freewheels the cover plate unscrews clockwise, so be careful about finding which way yours loosens. Just loosen it enough to unscrew by hand, then remove the freewheel from the hub. For this you'll have to use a tool designed specifically for the make and model freewheel you have. This operation might look simple, but it can ruin the freewheel before you even have it off the wheel.

Take the quick-release skewer cone off (if your bike has this feature) or the axle nut that holds the wheel on the bike. Place the tool on the axle and slide it down until is has full contact with the slots of the freewheel body. Screw the quick-release cone back on snugly against the tool, making sure the tool mates with the freewheel body. Any discrepancy in the fit of the tool with the body at this point should be corrected before proceeding any further. If it's not, the tool can strip the slots on the freewheel body rendering it unremovable unless you completely dismantle the freewheel every time you want to take it off the hub.

If the remover tool is completely engaged and fits well, put your largest wrench on the tool and carefully apply pressure parallel to the plane of the cogs. Don't cock the wrench over and watch to see if the remover slips out of the slots of the body. If grease was not applied at the factory before the freewheel was screwed onto the hub, the first attempt sometimes requires a bit more pressure than subsequent removals.

After the freewheel is removed, wipe all the excess grease off, and mount it onto the freewheel vise. Then take the pin wrench and unscrew the cover plate. Hold up the back part of the body with your fingers until you have the cover plate completely removed, so you don't lose the ball bearings. Count the number of bearings in the outer race of the freewheel, then carefully lift the entire assembly off the vise by lifting from the bottom where you've had your fingers all this time. Turn the unit upside down into a container to catch all those loose ball bearings. Also keep track of any shims that might be under the cover plate. Now slowly turn the unit over so the back of the unit is on the bottom again, and slowly let the inner body out far enough to let the rest of the bearings drop into the same container. Be careful not to pull it out any farther than necessary at this point so the pawls and springs remain intact. Carefully pull the inner body out of the rest of the unit and note carefully how the springs and pawls fit into your unit. Be very careful that the springs don't fly off someplace where you won't be able to find them. Sometimes the pivot slots of the pawls will be worn and the pawls themselves will go flying if you're not careful.

After the inner and outer body are separated, disassemble the pawls and spring (the springs on the Maeda unit aren't removable unless the pins are drilled out) and wash down the whole works in some solvent. After drying, take a look at the parts and see if any are worn or on the rough side. If any of the parts are worn, check your local bike shop to see if the required parts are available. If not, then you'll have to hunt around a bit or settle for a new freewheel. That's what I normally do. I keep the old ones for spare parts, as a new one doesn't cost that much unless you're buying the exotic alloy ones.

Why do I bother to take them apart? I do this with new freewheels to see if there is any roughness in the machining of the moving parts, and then try to improve the smoothness of the unit. This roughness is more prevalent in the less expensive units, although I've seen sloppy expensive units, too. If there is any roughness, a little work on the offending part with a small fine file and very fine emery cloth such as 000 grade will usually do the trick. Be careful with the filing and emery cloth as the parts, except for the pawls, are just case hardened and too much filing will take all of the surface hardening off and put you into the softer parent metal.

The reassembly of the body sometimes gets tricky, depending on what make you have. On the Maeda units it's a simple procedure. Just reassemble the spring and pawl assembly, being careful with the springs so they don't get bent, thus decreasing the tension so much that the pawls don't engage properly. But don't increase the tension either, or the ratchet will wear excessively. Put the inner body into the outer body without the bearings until you feel the pawls bottom out, then give the inner body a twist until the pawls engage. Now pull the inner body partially out again—just far enough so the rear bearings can be inserted. Drop the bearings into the rear race until you fill it up. (Use new bearings if you're rebuilding an older unit.) I advocate a full race. Some manufacturers don't fill their races up so the outer body rotates eccentrically to help pick the chain up when shifting. But unless the gear difference is four teeth or more, it won't matter, and even then I'm doubtful of how much it helps.

The washers should be replaced. The Maedas have the keyed washer installed first; the nonkeyed washers follow. Next fill the front race and replace the cover plate. After tightening the cover plate, see if there's any play or stiffness as the new balls are full diameter and an additional washer must be installed to shim the extra clearance for the bigger bearings. On the other hand, the races might be worn to the point where the extra washer/shim might not be required, so try it and subtract or add the washer as needed. After it's all reassembled, squirt some oil into the front and rear races, just enough to lubricate the bearings and ratchet assembly adequately.

If the freewheel you have is an exceptional one, and the body is still in good shape but the gears are beginning to develop a hook from chain wear, then you may want to replace both chain and freewheel. For replacing the cogs, use the chain wrench. Don't bother to cinch the last gear down when you replace it, as the first time on the bike afterwards will tighten it.

When reinstalling the freewheel on the hub, be sure to smear some grease on the hub threads so you can get it off easily next time.

Polishing Alloy Parts

Have you ever asked yourself why Campagnolo equipment is more expensive than other brands of equipment? Surely it's not the design because if the other brands were inferior they wouldn't stand up and would have more failures. The materials used in their manufacture are the same and the weights are comparable. The accuracy of the machined surfaces are within tolerances of precision parts, also. So what is it?

The biggest reason for the difference in price is in the time that Campagnolo spends to achieve the superior finish in its products. All the casting marks of their alloy parts have been carefully removed, any filing or grinding marks taken off and each piece carefully polished to a high luster and then anodized. The dull satin finish is a result of the anodizing process. The polished mirrorlike finish looks fantastic even before the anodizing process, and it's easier to maintain. It also forms a protective coating which resists corrosion to a greater degree than parts not finished as well. It also strengthens the part by removing any surface cracks which invariably develop into major cracks and failure in alloy equipment.

Even with the higher price tag some of us are still willing to pay the difference for the quality; except when it comes to brakes. Campagnolo sidepulls sell for as high as $75 to $80 for a complete setup and the majority of us, even those of us used to the higher price of other Campagnolo components, will balk at the cost of a pair of Campagnolo brakes. So we settle for another brand. I've chosen the Univeral 68 centerpulls, simply as an example. These brakes are excellent, but their finish leaves quite a bit to be desired. In fact, as far as the factory finishes on brakes are concerned, the Weinmann alloy brakes have a better finish. However, considering the going price of a set of Universals as only a quarter of the cost of a set of Campagnolos, it's some consolation.

What I did to my set of Universal centerpulls has not made it work any better, but it has a finish comparable, if not better looking, than a pair of Campagnolos, and it's a lot easier to keep clean. It's not a difficult process but it is time-consuming and tedious. However, after it was finished, I felt it was well worth the effort.

The first thing to do is to disassemble one of your brakes; do only one at a time to give yourself a guide in reassembling the first set. Then take a small fine file, a jeweler's file if you have one, and file off all the casting marks and small nicks and pits; easy does it or you'll end up with flat spots. After that take some 320-grit emery cloth and go over each entire alloy part, making sure that all the file marks have been removed. When you are satisfied with the degree of removal of the casting and file marks, take some jeweler's rouge on a soft cotton cloth and start polishing. You'll probably find that with the first piece you haven't gone over as thoroughly as you thought—just go over the piece with some more filing, then the emery cloth. If the scratches aren't too bad, the emery cloth and rouge will probably do. Try to keep the filing and emery cloth polishing going in one direction if possible as it will give you a better looking job in the end.

When you've completed the polishing with the jeweler's rouge, take some ordinary silver polish with some oxidation resistant compound or just ordinary car wax and apply a layer of it to the part to further protect it. All that's left now is to reassemble the brakes and install them on the bike.

This polishing process is especially effective on brakes because for some reason the manufacturers of brakes don't seem to finish off their products as well as crank and chainwheel manufacturers. The polishing process can be used on any other alloy parts such as stems, bars and hubs, which eventually receive nicks and scratches through normal usage.